Sam and the Sugar Bug

Written by: Dr. Humairah Shah
Illustrations by: Javier C Gonzalez III

This Book Belongs to:

Sam and the Sugar Bug
Copyright © 2015 Humairah Shah. All rights reserved.

ISBN: 978-0-9964911-1-2

Leila had been taking good care of her teeth. She would always brush her teeth in the morning and at night before going to bed. Leila's brother, Sam, would sometimes get lazy and forget to brush his teeth, especially at night.

One night, Sam had dinner and went to sleep without brushing his teeth. Randy, the evil sugar bug, was looking for food and was very hungry. Randy snuck into Leila's room and found nothing. Randy went from room to room looking for food, until at last he entered Sam's room.

"I smell food," said Randy, with an evil grin.

Evil Randy followed the scent and it led him to Sam's mouth. Randy jumped into Sam's mouth and said, "I am going to have a feast tonight! There is lots of food sticking to these teeth!" Randy had dinner and now he was full of energy. He decided that he would stay in Sam's mouth. Now he did not have to go looking for food every night. Randy started building his new home in Sam's teeth.

In the morning, Sam brushed his teeth in a hurry. If Sam had brushed long enough, he might have been able to kick evil Randy out of his mouth. Now Randy had more time to work on building his home in Sam's mouth and he grew stronger and stronger with all the food he was getting.

One night, after Sam fell asleep, Randy invited his friends to his home. They had a big party in Sam's mouth. Suddenly, Sam's tooth began to hurt. Sam woke up in pain.

"Mommy my mouth hurts," Sam cried.

Poor Sam was up all night. The next day, Sam's mom took him to Dr. Jane.

Dr. Jane looked at Sam's teeth with her magic mirror and was upset with what she saw. Randy and his friends were playing in Sam's teeth. Dr. Jane told Sam and his mother what she had found.

"That is why your teeth hurt," explained Dr. Jane.

"I will clean your teeth and get rid of Randy and his friends," said Dr. Jane. She used her magic whistle to spray lots of water into Sam's mouth. The sugar bugs felt the house shake and soon it was full of water. Randy and his friends were scared and had no idea what was happening.

They tried to escape but Dr. Jane and Suzie, the nurse, were quick to catch them. They found them hiding in the corner of the house. One by one, Dr. Jane and Suzie got rid of all the bugs. Dr. Jane fixed and filled all the holes that naughty Randy had dug in Sam's teeth.

Sam was happy that Randy and his friends no longer lived in his mouth. From that day on, he always brushed his teeth long enough to remove all the food. Sam brushed for two minutes every morning and every night, and he never let sugar bugs get into his mouth again.

Don't forget to floss,
I love hiding between
the teeth.

— Randy

Other Books by the Author

Funny Teeth and Bunny Ears a story about thumbsucking, follows Charlie and Marlie on their wild adventure! Despite their mother's warnings they continue to suck their thumbs. The two find themselves in a pickle as the story unfolds!

Leila and the Tooth Fairy is a story that every parent would love to read to their kids when they lose their teeth. The book allows them to save the dates each time they lose a tooth. The story takes the kids to a magical Tooth Fairy Land, and in a fun and easy way educates them about eating a healthy diet.

Leila's First Visit to the Dentist prepares children for their very first dental examination. It is a story that is intended to eliminate the fear of the unknown and make the trip to the dental office more enjoyable.

Made in the USA
San Bernardino, CA
05 March 2017